A beautiful photo book of book of British Garden Birds

House Sparrow

Blackbird

European Crested Tit

Chaffinch

Great Tit

Common Starling

Long Tailed Tit

Robin

Goldfinch

Blue Tit

Pigeon

White Dove

Coal Tit

Eurasian Bullfinch

Song Thrush

Starling

European Goldfinch

Great Spotted Woodpecker

Raven

Barn Owl

Jackdaw

Eurasian Jay

Fieldfare

Wren

Nuthatch

Redwing

Swallow

Whitethroat

Cuckoo

Dunnock

Greenfinch

Goldcrest

Willow Tit

Brambling

Mistle Thrush

Common Chiffchaff

Eurasian Siskin

Willow Warbler

Common Reed Bunting

Common Firecrest

Printed in Great Britain
by Amazon

23112266R00025